Dar  Boss of the Road

Written by
Jill Atkins

Illustrated by
Leo Trinidad

This is Darth.

He is big with long, thin arms and legs and a thick neck.

Look at him march up and down with his big chin in the air.

"I am the boss of this road," he yells.

Chan, Martha and Gareth are not as big as Darth.

Look at him rush up to them.

"I am rich!" Darth tells them. "And I am much bigger than you."

Chan, Martha and Gareth look up at Darth.

Darth chucks Chan's bat in the air.

He chucks Martha's hat in the rubbish bin.

He chucks Gareth's boots up on to a shed roof.

But then Darth gets a shock.

A turnip hits him on his ear.

"Ow!" he yells. "That hurts such a lot!"

He sits down on a chair
as tears run down his chin.

"Boo hoo!" he sobs.

Chan, Martha and Gareth look down at him.

Is this the big bad Darth?

"He is big, but perhaps he is not bad," Chan tells Gareth.

"If he gets the things back for us, he will be good," Martha tells Chan.

"I am not the boss of the road," Darth tells them.

He gets the bat for Chan.

Then he gets the hat for Martha and the boots for Gareth.

Now Darth, Chan, Martha and Gareth are all good chums!